SPOTLIGHT ON
THE SECOND WORLD WAR

Nathaniel Harris

SPOTLIGHT ON HISTORY

Spotlight on the Age of Exploration and Discovery
Spotlight on the Age of Revolution
Spotlight on Elizabethan England
Spotlight on the First World War
Spotlight on the Industrial Revolution
Spotlight on Post-War Europe
Spotlight on the Second World War
Spotlight on the Victorians

First published in 1985 by
Wayland (Publishers) Ltd
49 Lansdowne Place, Hove
East Sussex BN3 1HF, England

© Copyright 1985 Wayland (Publishers) Ltd

ISBN 0 85078 555 3

Typeset, printed and bound in the UK by
The Pitman Press, Bath

CONTENTS

1 THE ORIGINS OF THE WAR

The Second World War was the greatest conflict in human history, and raged over vast areas of the earth's surface. But it began in Europe, and many of its causes can be traced back to the way in which European affairs were settled after the First World War of 1914–18.

Europe after the First World War

In that war, Britain, France and the USA had defeated Germany and her allies. The main peace treaty, signed in 1919 at Versailles in France, forced the Germans to accept the entire blame for the war and

The French Marshal Foch and other Allied leaders outside the railway carriage in which the armistice was signed, ending the hostilities of the First World War.

Mussolini (wearing the sash) and his followers during the March on Rome in 1922.

agree to pay large sums to their ex-enemies as compensation ('reparations'). Germany was forced to demilitarize the Rhineland and reduce her army to 100,000 men, and forbidden to manufacture tanks, military aircraft or artillery. She was punished and humiliated in various other ways that Germans deeply resented, not least of these being the loss of more than 13 per cent of her pre-war territory.

All of this was hardly in the interests of future peace, since Germany, though temporarily disarmed and impoverished, was still potentially the strongest power in Europe. Other countries, too—notably Italy and Japan—were dissatisfied with the peace settlement.

Still, another world war was not inevitable. A new democratic Germany, the Weimar Republic, managed to survive the economic and political upsets that followed the war, and seemed to be settling down as part of a democratic Europe. And there were other hopeful developments, notably the League of Nations, which was established under the Versailles treaty to promote international co-operation and ld war. One ominous sign, however, was the establishment of the first fascist dictatorship in Italy under Benito Mussolini. At the start of his 'March on Rome' in October 1922, Mussolini had told his Fascist supporters: 'Either the government will be given to us or we shall take it, descending upon Rome.' Although Mussolini's threats contained a large element of bluff, Italy's political leaders lost their nerve and he succeeded in having himself appointed Prime Minister. Within a few years he had abolished democracy and made himself dictator of Italy.

The rise of Fascism

The European order suffered a terrible blow from the Great Depression, a world-wide economic collapse that began in 1929. Germany was hit particularly badly, and by 1932 there were over five million Germans unemployed. Old resentments were revived, faith in the Weimar Republic was shaken, and many people turned to Adolf

Adolf Hitler addressing an enormous Nazi rally in Nuremburg in 1935.

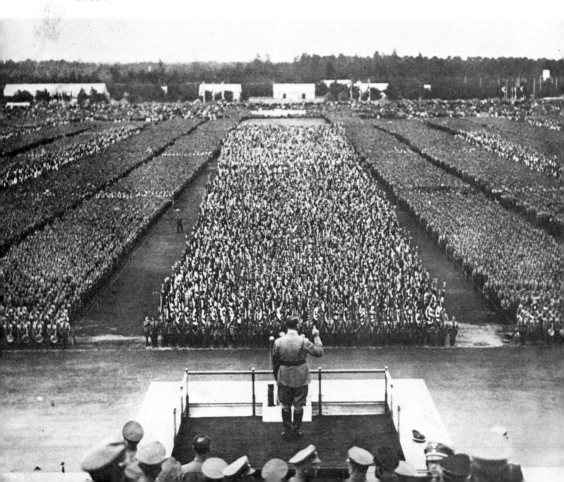

Hitler's Nazi (National Socialist) Party for salvation, and believed in his promise of 'the miracle of Germany's emergence as a nation'. Hitler took power in January 1933 and quickly turned Germany into a one-party state with himself as dictator; other political parties and free trade unions were banned, and opponents were imprisoned in brutal 'concentration' camps. The Weimar Republic disappeared and a new Germany, the Third Reich, was born.

Nazism, Italian Fascism and similar movements are often grouped together as 'fascist', since they had many similarities. Fascists were fiercely nationalistic and anti-democratic; they made a cult of leadership and obedience, militarizing the societies in which they lived and glorifying war as the noblest human activity. Nazism added its own peculiar racial element: Hitler proclaimed the Germans a superior 'master race', destined to rule 'sub-humans', such as the Slav peoples of Eastern Europe, and to eliminate the Jews, whom Nazis blamed for most of Germany's ills. In time, these weird irrational ideas were to have tragic consequences.

The darkening scene
In the 1930s it began to seem as though a new Dark Age was beginning. A barbaric militarism triumphed again and again. Germany and Italy committed acts of aggression that the League of Nations proved powerless to check. In Spain, General Francisco Franco, with

Republican soldiers fighting against General Franco's Nationalists during the Spanish Civil War of 1936–39.

German and Italian aid, defeated the elected government in a savage civil war, and set up a Fascist regime. Dictators flourished in a number of smaller countries, and on the other side of the world, a militaristic Japan took over Manchuria and launched an all-out attack on China.

The Fascist leaders were encouraged by the apparent weakness of

Joseph Stalin, general secretary of the Communist Party of the USSR from 1922 to 1935, and effectively the country's dictator.

the Western democracies. The United States had adopted a policy of 'Isolationism'. She had refused to ratify the Treaty of Versailles, and thus played no part in the League of Nations. Britain and France were slow to act, since they were reluctant to face the possibility of another war. They were half-hearted in condemning the Italian attack on the almost helpless African state of Abyssinia (modern Ethiopia) in 1935, and even tried to buy off the Italians with a slice of Abyssinian territory. Both Britain and France also refused to help the Spanish Republic.

The only country that did help Spain was the Soviet Union. This was the world's first Communist state, set up after the October Revolution of 1917. Communism promised a form of socialist society, planned and run for the common good, where—unlike the capitalist West—there would be no wealthy privileged class. At a time of poverty, unemployment and economic depression, the promise was an attractive one, and Communist parties sprang up in many countries, preaching revolution and following the 'party line' laid down by the USSR. Inevitably, British, French and other governments hated Communism and were reluctant to make common cause against Fascism with the USSR, which remained dangerously isolated. In truth, the reality of Soviet Communism was less appealing than its theory, and in practice the USSR was a one-party state under the ruthless dictatorship of Joseph Stalin. At a terrible cost in human suffering, he was wiping out all opposition and forcing through measures to transform backward Russia into a modern industrial society.

The road to war
By the late 1930s it had become clear that Germany was the chief threat to European peace. Hitler made his first important move in 1936, when he sent troops into the Rhineland, a part of Germany which had been demilitarized under the provisions of the Versailles treaty. He claimed to be acting in accordance with 'the fundamental right of a nation to secure its frontiers and ensure its possibilities of defence.' This was a gamble on Hitler's part, since the German army was still relatively weak. But Britain and France did nothing, and many people even felt that the Germans were acting within their rights. The same arguments were used when, in March 1938, Hitler brought Austria into a union (*Anschlüss*) with Germany, for the Austrians were a German-speaking people and appeared to be overwhelmingly in favour of a 'Greater Germany'.

Later in 1938, Hitler began to threaten Czechoslovakia, claiming that the Czechs were persecuting the large German minority in the country. By this time, people like Winston Churchill in Britain had become convinced that Hitler would keep finding excuses for aggres-

German troops re-occupy the Rhineland in 1936.

sion until he was opposed with force. But a majority in Britain and France still wanted peace at almost any price, and the British Prime Minister, Neville Chamberlain, took the lead in negotiating with Hitler. Eventually, a conference took place at Munich in Germany between Hitler, Mussolini, Chamberlain and the French premier, Daladier. To his surprise, Hitler got everything he wanted—possession of the Sudetenland, a large slice of Czechoslovakia that left the rest of the country defenceless. He now felt certain that Britain and France would always be too spineless to fight—while Chamberlain believed that his conciliatory policy, 'Appeasement', had brought 'peace in our time . . . peace with honour.' Churchill, on the other hand, declared: 'We have passed an awful milestone in our history, when the whole equilibrium of Europe has been deranged.'

Chamberlain was soon disillusioned. Within a few months Hitler had bullied the Czechs into accepting a 'protectorate' that put them under German control. In this case Hitler no longer had the excuse that he was rescuing his oppressed fellow-countrymen. Instead, he justified himself by saying: 'The statesmen who are opposed to us wish for peace . . . but they govern in countries whose domestic organization makes it possible that . . . they may lose their position to make way for others who are not anxious for peace . . . I have therefore decided . . .

to continue the construction of our fortifications in the West.'

Even Chamberlain now realized that German policy was incorrigibly aggressive. Like Germany, the democracies began to arm in earnest. Meanwhile, the shared expansionist aims of Germany, Italy and Japan brought them closer together, foreshadowing the eventual 'Axis' wartime alliance.

The final pre-war crisis began when Hitler threatened Poland, again claiming that the German minority was being mistreated. This time Britain and France took a firmer line and gave the Polish government guarantees of assistance in the event of German aggression. They also, rather lackadaisically, started negotiations for an alliance with the Soviet Union. However, the Germans got in first. In August 1939, despite the ideological differences between the two regimes, Germany and the USSR concluded a non-aggression pact. This was not an alliance, but an agreement that neither side would attack the other. For Hitler it meant that, in a war with Britain and France, Germany could rely on Russian neutrality and avoid having to fight on two fronts.

He now intensified his demands on Poland. Encouraged by the Western guarantees, the Poles rejected them. On 1 September 1939 German troops invaded Poland without any preliminary declaration of war.

Neville Chamberlain proclaims 'peace in our time' on his return from Munich.

The British and French honoured their guarantees. Britain sent an ultimatum to Germany demanding that she withdraw her forces from Poland. When this was refused, on 3 September Chamberlain addressed the British nation on the radio: 'I am speaking to you from the Cabinet Room at 10 Downing Street. This morning the British Ambassador in Berlin handed the German Government a final Note stating that unless we heard from them by 11 o'clock that they were prepared at once to withdraw their troops from Poland a state of war would exist between us. I have to tell you now that no such undertaking has been received, and that consequently this country is at war with Germany.'

Europe at the outbreak of war in 1939.

2 BLITZKRIEG

The destruction of Poland

Despite their declarations of war, the Allies (the British and French) did little to help the Poles. An immediate offensive in the West might well have ended the war while the German army was tied up in Poland. But both now and later the Allies overestimated the scale of German rearmament and the size of the Germany army. They were misled by German propaganda and by their own fears.

Although large, Poland was not a major military power, and a German victory was a foregone conclusion. But the speed of the Polish collapse should have alerted the Allies to the effectiveness of the German military machine. The Luftwaffe (German airforce) struck at Polish airfields and eliminated the Polish air force within 48 hours. German armies invaded from several directions, heading for Warsaw. In every case, the first thrust was made by their armour—above all,

A German Stuka dive-bomber in action.

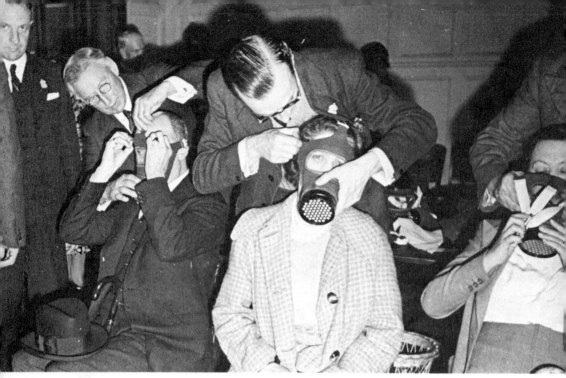

British civilians are trained in the use of gas-masks.

their tanks, the Panzers—which broke through the enemy front and raced far ahead of the infantry, fanning out. Reinforced by dive-bombing and strafing Stuka planes, the rampaging tanks disrupted the Poles' lines of communication and the coordination of their armies. With the Polish forces in a state of confusion, the arrival of the German infantry and artillery clinched victory.

This was a new style of offensive which the Germans called *Blitzkrieg*—'lightning warfare'. By the middle of September the Poles had been defeated, though Warsaw, the capital, held out until the 27th. Even before this, on the 17th, Soviet forces had entered eastern Poland, and the country was then partitioned between the USSR and Germany. Poland simply ceased to exist.

Phoney war?

During the winter of 1939–40 there was still no fighting between Allied and German forces on the Western front. The German General Keitel later said: 'We had always expected an attack by the French during the Polish campaign and were very surprised that nothing happened.' American journalists talked of 'the Phoney War', and hinted that there might be a negotiated peace. The Germans called it the *Sitzkrieg*—the 'sitting-down war'. In Britain, food rationing had been introduced and gas-masks issued to protect the public from expected gas attacks from the air. But the attacks never came.

Although the British troops in France—the British Expeditionary Force (BEF)—steadily increased in number, Allied strategy remained defensive. The French had built a great chain of fortifications that was believed to be impregnable: the Maginot Line, which stretched along their eastern border from Switzerland to Belgium, leaving only the Belgian border in need of defence by mobile units. Understandably, this encouraged a confident but passive outlook in the French. The British were equally unwilling to take risks, believing they could win the war through an economic blockade of Germany.

Even in 1939 this looked over-optimistic. German submarines, the U-boats, began to sink Allied shipping, and a German battleship, the *Graf Spee*, ranged the South Atlantic destroying merchant vessels. In December, however, British ships hunted down the *Graf Spee* and damaged her so badly that her captain scuttled her in the port of neutral Montevideo (Uruguay). Britain still ruled at least the surface of the waves.

The most active power during the Phoney War was the USSR, which brought the Baltic states of Lithuania, Latvia and Estonia under her unwelcome 'protection'. She also demanded territorial concessions and military bases from the Finns. When they refused, they were battered into submission—although only after the Red Army had suffered huge casualties and revealed a startling military inefficiency. These acquisitions, along with eastern Poland, gave the Russians a buffer zone which they hoped might absorb the first shock of a future German attack.

German soldiers disembark on the Norwegian shore on 9 April 1940.

War in the North

The Phoney War ended on 9 April 1940, when German naval forces entered the fjord (inlet) leading to Oslo, the capital of Norway. The Norwegian government was given an ultimatum declaring that 'German military operations aim exclusively at protecting the north against the proposed occupation of Norwegian bases by Anglo-French forces', and warning that 'resistance would lead only to futile bloodshed.' The Norwegians did resist, but German parachutists successfully occupied Oslo, and there were naval landings at other points on the coast. At the same time, German troops moved into Denmark and occupied it after only token resistance. All of this was achieved in a single day.

Wrecked shipping in Narvik Bay after a British attack.

Only the ruins of a church remain standing above ground in one area of Rotterdam after German bombing.

Both conquered countries were neutral, but their geographical position at the mouth of the Baltic made them inevitable targets in a ruthlessly fought world war. Furthermore, any power controlling Norway could interfere with the passage of vital supplies of iron ore from neutral Sweden to Germany—as in fact the Allies had hoped to do. They had also mined Norwegian coastal waters just before the German invasion, recognizing their naval potential. The Germans were more ruthless, but neither side had completely clean hands.

Allied troops landed to help the Norwegians, and the German conquest was not easy. The British navy took a heavy toll of German shipping, and in the far north, at Narvik, the invaders were cut off. An Allied expedition established itself in the town so successfully that it was only withdrawn in June, when the Allies had met disaster elsewhere.

The fall of France
On 10 May 1940, German troops poured across the frontiers of neutral Holland and Belgium, by-passing the Maginot Line. The Allies had expected this, and they advanced to help the Dutch and Belgians. But

the impact of the German attack was such that they had no time to dig in. Holland fell in four days, though not before Rotterdam had suffered a devastating air attack. In Belgium the Allied armies fell back, shaken but still expecting to stabilize the battle line as they had done during the First World War.

Then the Germans launched their main attack. They came through the Ardennes—forest country that the Allies wrongly believed to be impassable by motorized units. Facing only light opposition, the German armour roared all the way across northern France, reaching the sea on 21 May and cutting off the Allied retreat from the south. Retreat quickly turned into disaster. By late May, over 600,000 Allied troops were boxed in round the Channel port of Dunkirk and seemed on the point of destruction. Hitler was described by one of his generals as being 'beside himself with joy'.

Then the 'miracle of Dunkirk' occurred: hundreds of ships, large and small, sailed out from English ports and succeeded in rescuing about 340,000 Allied troops before Dunkirk fell. Huge quantities of equipment and many ships were lost, but complete disaster had at least been avoided.

Long lines of British troops waiting to be evacuated from the beaches of Dunkirk.

German artillery passing under the Arc de Triomphe in Paris in June 1940.

France could not be saved. On 5 June the Germans launched their drive south. By this stage of the campaign they were even superior in numbers, but again their *Blitzkrieg* tactics brought victory in an astonishingly short time. And although some French units fought bravely, the country was demoralized, even at government level.

On 16 June Marshal Pétain became Prime Minister of France. Although one of the heroes of the First World War, he was now deeply defeatist. He immediately asked the Germans for an armistice—in effect, terms for a surrender—which was signed on 22 June. German forces retained control of northern France and the Atlantic seaboard. 'Independent' France, governed from the small spa town of Vichy, was remodelled by Pétain into a semi-fascist authoritarian state, tolerated by Germany while it 'co-operated'.

On 10 June, when France was clearly on the verge of defeat, Italy entered the war on the German side—uninvited. Mussolini, once Europe's leading Fascist dictator, had long felt overshadowed by Hitler. While Austria and Czechoslovakia were being effortlessly swallowed by the Third Reich, Mussolini had only managed to overrun little Albania. At the outbreak of war, Italy had remained neutral, but now that a German victory seemed assured, Mussolini wanted to share the spoils.

It was a mistake. Italy was not a major power, although Mussolini's personality had for years made people believe otherwise. The Italian army, ill-equipped and ill-prepared, failed even to defeat the weak French units on the Franco-Italian border—the first of many Italian humiliations. In time, Hitler was to find the Italian alliance a distinct liability.

Mussolini and Hitler acknowledge the cheers of a German crowd.

3 THE ENEMY AT THE DOOR

Nobody would have been surprised if Britain had begun negotiations for peace with Germany at the end of June 1940. If the German army succeeded in crossing the Channel, its victory was a certainty; and even if Britain survived, Hitler's grip on the Continent seemed unbreakable.

Britain fights on

But the British were determined to fight on, and had found a leader who shared and expressed their determination. Winston Churchill had replaced Neville Chamberlain as Prime Minister on 10 May—coincidentally, the day on which the Germans attacked Belgium and Holland. He told the House of Commons, 'I have nothing to offer but

Winston Churchill with navy, army and air force chiefs.

blood, toil, tears and sweat ... You ask, What is our aim? I can answer in one word: Victory.' On the radio, the universal medium of the time, Churchill's old-fashioned eloquence was curiously effective and inspiring, stiffening the British will to endure and resist.

Britain's resolve was shown by her treatment of the French navy. She was not at war with Vichy France, but her safety depended on the continued supremacy of the Royal Navy—and Churchill was not prepared to risk a possible German takeover of the French fleet. On 3 July French ships in British ports were seized, and when a fleet at Oran in North Africa refused to surrender, it was ruthlessly destroyed by British naval aircraft.

Not all Frenchmen accepted the German victory. General Charles de Gaulle defied Vichy and set up a 'Free French' government in London. Refugees from other conquered countries also organized governments-in-exile, and Poles, Czechs, Norwegians and others fought with or in the British armed forces. The dominions, or Commonwealth countries of Canada, Australia, New Zealand and South Africa, stood by Britain, which also controlled a large colonial empire, including India, and 'protected' states such as Egypt.

General Charles de Gaulle meets members of the Home Guard during his exile in England.

American eggs, sent under the terms of the Lend-Lease Act, are unloaded at a British port.

Britain had a major but 'invisible' ally in the United States. Most Americans sympathized with the Allied cause but were quite determined to stay out of the war. However, their president, Franklin D. Roosevelt, who was to describe the USA as 'the arsenal of the democracies', helped to re-equip Britain after Dunkirk. In March 1941, he persuaded Congress to approve the Lend-Lease Act. In effect, the United States decided to supply beleaguered Britain on a huge scale without being paid until after the war.

None of this would have mattered if the Germans had been able to invade Britain. The invasion plan ('Operation Sea Lion') existed, and barges and troops were concentrated in the Channel ports. Churchill, speaking of the invasion threat, declared: 'We shall defend every village, every town and every city. The vast mass of London itself, fought street by street, could easily devour an entire hostile army; and we would rather see London laid in ruins and ashes than that it should be tamely and abjectly enslaved.' But the German navy, depleted by its losses in Norway, could not match the British fleet, and an invasion would be doubly risky without assured superiority in the air. To obtain this, the Germans launched 'the Battle of Britain'.

In July 1940, the *Luftwaffe* had concentrated about 1,000 bombers and 1,000 fighter planes in northern France; the Royal Air Force (RAF) faced them with about 700 fighters. However, the RAF did have compensating advantages: it had developed a radar system to give early warning of the enemy's approach; its new fighter plane, the Spitfire, was a better machine than its German rival, the Messerschmitt 109; and it was fighting within its own airspace.

The Battle of Britain

The *Luftwaffe* began by attacking shipping and coastal ports, then switched to the factories and airfields of south-east England, bringing about a head-on conflict with the RAF. The Battle of Britain reached its height in late August and early September 1940. The RAF emerged victorious, but came close to collapse, largely because it was losing pilots much faster than replacements could be trained. The few experienced pilots who did survive became totally exhausted, and it seemed that only will-power kept them going. One of them later wrote: 'We were dead ... too tired even to get drunk.' Winston Churchill thanked the fighter pilots with the words: 'Never in the field of human conflict was so much owed by so many to so few.'

On 7 September the Germans adopted new tactics. Almost a thousand planes took to the air and carried out a bombing raid on London. Provoked by British bombing of Berlin, and over-estimating the remaining strength of the RAF, the Germans broke off the direct battle in the air and set out to destroy Britain's cities and terrorize her population. We can now see that this was a mistake. It gave the RAF time to recover, and within a few weeks it had established such a complete superiority over the *Luftwaffe* that the German bombers began to attack only under cover of night.

Two German Dornier bombers high over London at the start of the air-raid of 7 September 1940.

A group of Londoners posing in front of their bombed-out homes in the East End.

Nevertheless, over the next few months the 'Blitz' seemed devastating. Blazes in London, Coventry and other cities lit up the night sky, while thousands of people took refuge in air-raid shelters and underground stations. London was bombed relentlessly—every night from 7 September to 2 November, and then only a little less frequently when some German bombers were diverted to attack provincial cities. Some parts of the capital suffered particularly badly. The author Vera Brittain described an area in the East End in these terms: 'All life, all semblance of human habitation has disappeared from these crushed and flattened acres.'

Children were evacuated to the countryside to protect them from the bombing, but many of the less fortunate city dwellers who remained were killed or maimed by bomb blasts or buried under falling masonry. However, although the damage and loss of life were substantial, the Blitz actually demonstrated the limited effectiveness of bombing. The results were simply not proportionate to the effort involved. At the end of the Blitz, the morale of the British people remained unbroken, and the country was more thoroughly organized for war than ever before in its history; the civilian British had become a nation of factory workers, land girls, air-raid wardens and members of 'Dad's Army', the Home Guard recruited from the elderly and the unfit.

Bismarck, *Germany's finest battleship, firing on a British warship. A few days later,* Bismarck *was sunk.*

At the time when the Blitz was at its height, between September 1940 and May 1941, the war at sea was beginning to assume serious proportions. The main threat was to Britain's merchant shipping from U-boats operating from the Atlantic harbours of Norway and France. Doenitz, the German Admiral, declared: 'The U-boat will always be the backbone of warfare against England,' and, by the end of 1940, more than 4,500,000 tons of Allied and neutral shipping had been sunk in the Atlantic. Churchill later wrote: 'The only thing that ever frightened me during the war was the U-boat peril.' Germany's surface fleet was less effective, and even her finest battleship, the *Bismarck*, was only used as a raider, although it did considerable damage before being hunted down and sunk in May 1941.

The first Axis setbacks
The German grip on Eastern Europe tightened during the winter of 1940–41, as Hungary, Romania and Bulgaria were bullied or cajoled into joining the Axis.

The spread of the war into the Mediterranean brought the first setbacks. In late October 1940 the Italians attacked Greece from occupied Albania—and a few weeks later found themselves being pushed back across the mountains by the small Greek army. In Africa, where large Italian armies were established in their colonies in Libya, Abyssinia and Somalia, attacks on the much smaller British and Commonwealth forces achieved some successes. Then, to the surprise of the Allies themselves, a counter-attack launched by General Wavell turned into a triumphal march. Huge numbers of prisoners were taken and the conquest of Libya seemed imminent. But new developments in the Balkans—and a further extension of the field of war—changed the situation again.

4 THE WORLD AT WAR

Early in 1941, the Second World War was still far from being global in reality. Apart from much of Europe and parts of North Africa, the majority of the Earth's surface remained unscathed. However, this situation was to change dramatically during 1941.

Conflict in the Mediterranean

Mussolini's failures eventually forced Hitler to commit his troops to the Mediterranean. Under pressure, Yugoslavia agreed to join the Axis but then changed her mind. A furious Hitler ordered an invasion which began on 6 April 1941. Simultaneously German units in Bulgaria burst into Greece, where 60,000 British troops had been landed.

The *Blitzkrieg* again proved irresistible. Yugoslavia capitulated on 17 April. The British, driven back before they managed to dig in, had to be lifted off by the navy while the *Luftwaffe* pounded them

Paratroops drop and a plane crashes during the German airborne invasion of Crete.

relentlessly. In May the Germans captured Crete from Allied and Greek troops after spectacular but costly airborne landings. This was the first successful airborne invasion in history; but the German paratroop corps never really recovered from the losses it sustained.

For Britain, the consequences of these defeats were more serious. Naval losses during the evacuations eroded the superiority which had been established over the Italian fleet in the Mediterranean in engagements at Taranto and Cape Matapan. The presence of the *Luftwaffe* in the Mediterranean now posed an additional threat. Furthermore, the diversion of troops to Greece led to the calling-off of the successful Libyan offensive, giving the Germans time to intervene. General Erwin Rommel was sent to North Africa with two Panzer divisions—supposedly just enough to bolster the demoralized Italians. While Wavell, the British Commander-in-Chief, was signalling to his High Command on 30 March, 'I do not believe that he [Rommel] can make any big effort for another month,' Rommel had decided that 'speed is the thing that matters here.' Accordingly, the tanks of the German Afrika Korps attacked and routed the British, and by mid-April 1941 Axis forces had again reached the Egyptian border.

The disasters in Greece and North Africa endangered the entire British position in the Eastern Mediterranean. The only consolations were in East Africa, where Commonwealth forces defeated the Italians and restored Abyssinian independence, and in the Middle East: in April, British forces overthrew a pro-German regime that had taken power in Iraq; in June, British and Free French troops captured Syria from Vichy; and in August, Iran was occupied by Britain and her new ally—the Soviet Union.

Operation Barbarossa

At three o'clock in the morning of 22 June 1941, without warning, Nazi Germany attacked the USSR. Three and a half million German, Romanian, Finnish and other Axis troops poured across the Soviet borders, quickly breaking through the Russian lines. Despite Stalin's preparations, the German attack seems to have taken him completely by surprise. Like other victims of the *Blitzkrieg*, Soviet soldiers were stunned by its speed and force. Stalin's only answer was to call upon the Russian people to 'scorch the earth' as they retreated. On 3 July, in a radio broadcast, he declared that 'All valuable property, including metals, grain, and fuel, that cannot be withdrawn, must be destroyed

Opposite *Rommel (on the right) surveys the North African desert from his command car.*

without fail.' In effect, he intended to yield space to buy time; the space yielded was to be made unusable to the advancing Germans. The Russians fought grimly enough in places, but were overwhelmed or outmanoeuvred; within a few weeks the Germans had taken over a million Russian prisoners and broken several Russian armies.

The attack on Russia—Operation Barbarossa—was the logical culmination of the Nazis' philosophy, which was fanatically anti-Communist and contemptuous of the Slavs as 'sub-human'. For Britain, the attack was good news: the Blitz lessened in intensity as the *Luftwaffe* was switched to the East, and Britain no longer stood alone in Europe. Winston Churchill, although a life-long hater of Communism, unhesitatingly embraced Stalin as an ally and friend. Soon British factories would be contributing to the Soviet war effort.

German vehicles move up towards the front as Russian prisoners are marched in the opposite direction, to the prison camps.

Scorched earth; German tanks pass a Russian farmhouse which was set ablaze to make it useless to the invaders.

The German army of 1941 must rank as one of the most effective in history, but the invasion was a bigger gamble than Hitler realized. Russia was vast, her population huge, her winter cruel; it had often been said that the best Russian commander was 'General Winter', whose past victims included the Grand Army of Napoleon. The Germans were well aware of this, but believed they could end the war in a single summer campaign. Six months before Operation Barbarossa began, Hitler had declared: 'The German Armed Forces must be prepared to crush Soviet Russia in a quick campaign before the end of the war against England.' Having smashed the Soviet armies, they would race on in three great waves, occupying Russia's industrial regions and taking her major cities: Leningrad in the north, Smolensk and Moscow in central Russia, and Kiev in the south. The Russians would be pushed right out of Europe, beyond the Ural Mountains.

It almost worked, and for a time the invasion was even ahead of schedule. The Panzers pressed on and on, victory followed victory. Smolensk fell in July; by September Kiev had been stormed and Leningrad was surrounded. But Moscow, the Soviet capital, was now the chief German objective. The German advance slowed down as the Russians continued, against all expectations, to produce fresh troops. And sheer distance began to take its toll, exhausting the infantry and wearing out motorized equipment. Stalin's 'scorched-earth' policy also ensured that German supply lines were stretched to the limit.

Still the advance went on; but time was running out. In a supreme effort the German army came within sight of Moscow in early December and prepared to encircle it with a 'pincer movement'. But before the pincer could close, General Winter struck—early and, as chance would have it, with almost unprecedented severity. The Germans, with only summer equipment, froze and came to a halt. On 6 December the Soviet Red Army launched a winter counter-offensive against the invader. Instead of the single short campaign they had envisaged, the Germans found themselves locked in a titanic struggle that was to end only with the war itself.

The day of infamy
On 7 December 1941, the day after the Russians began their counter-offensive, another great area of the globe was engulfed by war when carrier-borne Japanese planes attacked and crippled the US Pacific Fleet at its base, Pearl Harbor in the Hawaiian Islands. All eight US warships were sunk or damaged, over 150 aircraft were destroyed, and almost 2,400 Americans lost their lives. Like so many Axis aggressions, Japan's was a surprise attack undertaken without formal declaration of war. President Roosevelt labelled it 'a date which will live in infamy.' The Japanese followed up their advantage with a massive offensive in South-East Asia and the Western Pacific.

Relations between the United States and the European Axis powers had been stretched to the limit even before this. In August 1941, Roosevelt and Churchill had met on a battleship in mid-Atlantic, and issued the Atlantic Charter, which affirmed democratic values and explicitly condemned Nazi tyranny. The American navy had helped to protect British merchant shipping, and one US destroyer had even been sent to the bottom by a U-boat. Axis consulates in the United States had been closed and Lend-Lease extended to the Soviet Union. But American opinion remained opposed to open war.

The attack on Pearl Harbor made up the Americans' minds for them. They were at war. And four days later, Japan's allies, Germany and Italy, also declared war on the USA. The conflict was now truly world-wide.

Although Japan was attacking British colonies, and so adding

German troops trudging through the frozen Russian landscape in the winter of 1941.

The aftermath of Pearl Harbor; three of America's battleships lie damaged following the surprise Japanese attack.

greatly to Britain's difficulties, Churchill was overjoyed. He had no doubt that alliance with the USA would make all the difference: 'We had won the war. England would live . . . Hitler's fate was sealed.' He was clearly right: the enormous resources of 'the Grand Alliance'—Britain, the USSR, the USA—were bound to bring victory in the end. But in the short run it was different: the Axis was reaching the high point of its fortunes.

5 THE NEW ORDER

Early in 1942 there were one or two hopeful signs for the Allies. The Russian winter offensive had scored notable successes, and in North Africa the British, under their new commander, General Auchinleck, had driven Rommel back. The worst news came from the Far East, where the Japanese were everywhere victorious and seemed poised to attack British India and Australia.

The first German vehicles to enter Tobruk after the town was captured from the Allies in June 1942.

The high tide of Fascism

By the summer of 1942 the situation had deteriorated on the other fronts. In Russia, the German summer offensive swept through the Crimea, where Sevastopol fell in July after a heroic defence. Stalin ordered his men: 'Not a single step backward ... You have to fight to your last drop of blood to defend ... every foot of Soviet territory.' But the invaders crossed the Don and drove towards Stalingrad, a great industrial city on the Volga. Their main objective was the Caucasus, where there were great oilfields whose capture would fuel the Axis effort while depriving the Russians of a vital war material. By August, they had penetrated the Caucasus and appeared to be on the verge of success.

Rommel had begun a new offensive in the Western Desert as early as January 1942. It culminated in May with a major victory over British and French troops, followed by the capture of Tobruk, an Allied-held enclave on the Libyan coast. Rommel's subsequent thrust into Egypt went deeper than before, and the offensive was only halted in November at El Alamein, sixty miles from the vital supply port of Alexandria.

Elsewhere in the Mediterranean, German air strikes from Sicily and Sardinia battered the island of Malta, a strategically valuable British colony. Enduring bombardment and blockade, the Maltese were awarded a medal, the George Cross—an odd, unique recognition of collective heroism.

In the Atlantic, 'wolf packs' of U-boats were in full cry, destroying incredible quantities of Allied shipping carrying food and war materials across the ocean to Britain or on the 'Greenland run' to Russia's Arctic ports. Even the shipyards of the USA, working overtime, were failing to replace the losses fast enough.

For a moment, then, it seemed that Hitler's boasted 'Thousand-Year Reich' might endure, and along with it the 'New Order' he had imposed on Europe.

Hitler's Europe

The Reich was ruled by the National Socialist or Nazi Party, which tolerated no opposition. Its leaders included Herman Goering, Hitler's deputy and chief of the *Luftwaffe*, and Dr Josef Goebbels, minister of propaganda and master of 'the Big Lie'. As the war went on, both began to be overshadowed by Heinrich Himmler, chief of the sinister black-uniformed SS, which originated as Hitler's élite body-guard and eventually became a million-strong security force that terrorized Europe.

The SS swore allegiance not to Germany or the Party, but to Germany's all-powerful Führer (leader), Adolf Hitler. Each SS cadet

Hitler with two of his Nazi leaders, Josef Goebbels and Herman Goering.

swore an oath of honour:

> I swear to thee Adolf Hitler
> As Führer and Chancellor of the German Reich
> Loyalty and Bravery.
> I vow to thee and to the superiors of your choosing
> Obedience unto death
> So help me God.

As dictator of the victorious Reich, Hitler stamped his will on conquered Europe. The New Order was the direct expression of his philosophy— a crude philosophy which extolled ruthlessness, brutality and war. It pictured the Germans as a master race of 'Aryans'— roughly speaking, blonde-haired, blue-eyed types—who had every right to enslave or exterminate 'inferior' peoples.

Given this outlook, Germany had little to offer Europe except

Hitler, with a bodyguard of SS men, greets supporters in Berlin.

oppression. There was some pretence that a Nazi Europe represented civilization in conflict with a barbarous 'Asiatic' Russia, and this—or at least anti-Communism—did have some impact. But the realities of Nazi domination became increasingly clear. The resources of the occupied countries were plundered, and millions of men were conscripted to work in Germany. The New Order was intended to benefit the Reich alone.

In Eastern Europe, Nazi oppression was still more open, and unbelievably savage. Ultimately, Hitler aimed to provide *Lebensraum*—living space—for the German population by exterminating the 'sub-human' Slavs and colonizing Poland and European Russia with German settlers. As a first step, Slavs were treated with harshness—underfed, denied education, executed on the slightest excuse—and millions did in fact perish. The atrocities committed against the conquered Poles were systematic; atrocities against the Russians were habitual—including the murder of millions of Russian prisoners of war, deliberately worked to death in German factories. Inevitably, the Russians responded in kind, and the conflict in the East was conducted on both sides with a terrible ferocity.

The vilest of all Nazi policies were carried out in the concentration camps. Here, political prisoners and other 'undesirables' who escaped immediate execution were herded, hounded, subjected to ghastly

A prisoner in a German concentration camp.

'medical' experiments, and finally murdered. By late 1941 the murdering was systematized, as the Nazis devised ways of gassing thousands of victims every day. People of many nations suffered—the gypsies of Europe, for example, were virtually wiped out. But in terms of numbers, the Jews were the principal victims, crammed into cattle trucks and brought by train from all over the Continent to Auschwitz, Treblinka and other death camps in Eastern Europe. About six million are believed to have died. The whole story is one of the most revolting in history, and also one of the maddest: Germany, engaged in a life-or-death struggle, devoted men and resources to a crazy racial crusade against mostly powerless men, women and children.

Vidkun Quisling, leader of the Norwegian Government under the Nazis, salutes a visiting German officer.

Tito (on the right) with some of his partisans in the mountains of Yugoslavia.

Collaboration and resistance

The Nazis found a degree of support or co-operation in their conquered territories. Some 'collaborators' shared the Nazis' outlook—Vidkun Quisling, for example, who had led the Norwegian Nazi Party before the war, and in 1942 became prime minister of occupied Norway. 'Quisling' became a term of abuse for all collaborators. Other collaborators were influenced by anti-Communism, welcoming the German army as a bulwark against revolution. The Nazis were even able to recruit a foreign legion, composed of young men from all over Europe, to fight on the Eastern Front.

Many collaborators were simply opportunists, but there were also those who believed that as patriots they must make the best of things as they were. This was especially the case in Vichy France, nominally independent yet inevitably subservient to Germany. For many, prudent co-operation only slowly merged into collaboration, helping to round up Jews for transportation to the camps, and so on. And with the emergence of active resistance to the Nazis, those who had compromised were driven into closer collaboration and found themselves at war with their fellow-countrymen.

In the long run, Nazi brutality was self-defeating, and aroused widespread resistance. In the Ukraine, for example, Stalin's rule was distinctly unpopular, and the conquering Germans were actually welcomed—until the SS moved in and the murders began. Then Ukrainians, like other Soviet men and women, soon became partisans fighting behind the enemy's lines. In mountainous Yugoslavia, too, Communist partisans led by Tito became a formidable military threat; and in France, in areas where the terrain was favourable, the Maquis harrassed the Nazis and the Vichy militia, the Milice. Elsewhere, resistance was more clandestine, taking the form of sabotage or intelligence-gathering. British planes dropped small arms and other supplies to the Resistance, hoping to 'set Europe ablaze'. BBC broadcasts to occupied Europe, signalled by the dramatic drumbeats of Beethoven's 'knocking of fate', were listened to in secret by millions. German reprisals for acts of resistance were horrific, sometimes going as far as the murder of every man, woman and child in a village. Generally speaking, reprisals only provoked further resistance, which grew steadily in intensity as the high tide of Fascism began to ebb.

A Maquis patrol setting off on a raid against the Germans in the French Alps.

6 THE TURNING POINT

Axis triumphs during the spring and summer of 1942 concealed two decisively important facts. One was that the balance of men and resources had tilted sharply to the Allied side. The other was that the sheer scale of Axis conquests left them overextended, guarding too many territories and fighting on too many fronts. In North Africa, Rommel was undersupplied because the Russian front had priority; yet even in 1942, as the German armies thrust across the Don, the advantage in numbers and equipment was steadily passing to the Russians. In the Reich itself, civilians began to experience the terrors of war in May 1942, when the RAF launched a 'thousand-bomber raid' on Cologne as a prelude to a strategic bombing offensive that went on to the last day of the war.

As American industry adjusted to war production, her allies received vast quantities of food and war materials, despite the U-boats.

One new American warship slides down the slipway, shortly to be followed by another.

By the end of 1942 replacements of shipping were outrunning losses, and in 1943 the Battle of the Atlantic began to be won: U-boat bases were bombed and production of escort warships and aircraft increased to a point where the submarine menace began to be tamed.

The Japanese triumph was even shorter lived. In the course of 1942 their advance on Australia was frustrated, the battle of Midway ended their naval supremacy, and American troops began the bloody reconquest of the Solomon Islands.

The real turning point of the war, however, came in the autumn and winter of 1942–43.

Montgomery and other 'Desert Rats' in North Africa.

A German tank crew surrenders as British infantry advance during the battle of El Alamein.

Decision in North Africa

In July 1942 Lieutenant-General Bernard Montgomery took command of the British 8th Army, by now nicknamed 'the Desert Rats'. A few weeks later, Montgomery showed his quality by beating off a new Axis attack—helped by a knowledge of Rommel's resources and plans, provided by Britain's highly successful codebreakers.

Unlike his predecessors, Montgomery succeeded in resisting Churchill's impatient demands for an immediate offensive. Capitalizing on the Allies' material advantage, he waited until he had built up an overwhelming superiority. Then, on the night of 23–24 October 1942, hundreds of guns bombarded the Axis positions at El Alamein, and the Allies went in with twice as many men and tanks as the Axis forces. The Germans fought hard, and even counter-attacked, but after a twelve-day battle the Allies had won—all the more decisively because Hitler commanded Rommel to 'stand fast, yield not a yard of ground and throw every gun and every man into the battle,' when he might still have retreated in good order. As it was, the 8th Army chased the broken Afrika Korps all the way to Tunisia, and was unlucky not to catch 'the Desert Fox', Rommel, himself.

Meanwhile, in November, just after the battle of El Alamein, the Allies landed in three places much further west, on the coast of France's North African empire. The invaders were mainly American troops, facing their first significant actions in the West. The French forces remained loyal to Vichy and fought, but within a few days they were overwhelmed and capitulated in both Algeria and Morocco.

From this point it became easier to induce Frenchmen to change sides, since the German army, taking no chances, immediately occupied Vichy France. Pétain's government now functioned as nothing more than a German tool, and Frenchmen were left with a clear-cut choice between collaboration and resistance. Many chose resistance—notably the French navy at Toulon which, unable to escape in time, scuttled the fleet rather than let it fall into German hands.

The Germans and Italians decided to hang on in Tunisia, ferrying in troops via Sicily. In February 1943 they defeated the Americans at the battle of the Kasserine Pass, and they were only finally driven out in May 1943. Even after major disasters, the Axis would clearly not be easy to beat.

Disaster at Stalingrad

By November 1942 the German advance in the Caucasus had ground to a halt. The struggle now centred on Stalingrad. Hitler ordered its capture at all costs, while Stalin ordered that 'his' city (Stalingrad means 'Stalin City') should be held at all costs. Both sides poured in stupendous numbers of men, and Germans and Russians fought savagely, street by street.

The Germans inched forward slowly, but their gains proved illusory. Concentrating on the city, they left their flanks thinly defended by their Romanian allies. The Russians quietly massed fresh armies north and south of Stalingrad, and on 19 and 20 November smashed through on both sides. By the 21st the two arms of the Russian pincer had met, and the German invader was encircled. Despite terrible sufferings, the Germans held out through the winter. But on 2 February 1943 the frozen, starving remnants of twenty-two divisions surrendered.

If there was such a thing as a turning point in the course of the Second World War, it was Stalingrad. The USSR would survive, and in time the Allies would win. Even so, the Germans were still capable of halting the Russians, launching offensives and winning victories. But in July 1943 there was another catastrophe. Their offensive at Kursk found the Russians thoroughly prepared. With three thousand tanks on each side, Kursk was the greatest tank battle in history; and it was the nemesis of the German *Blitzkrieg*. After Kursk there was no longer any doubt: the Russians were winning.

Russian artillery in action in the ruins of a factory outside Stalingrad.

Italy knocked out

Roosevelt and Churchill celebrated victory in North Africa by meeting there in January 1943. At this, the Casablanca conference, Roosevelt declared his terms for ending the war—no terms at all, 'Unconditional Surrender'—and Churchill agreed.

In private, the Allied leaders made another important decision. The invasion of mainland Europe would be put off in favour of an attack on Sicily, since possession of the island would give the Allies complete control of the Mediterranean. A great amphibious landing on 10 July 1943 was followed by five weeks of hard fighting which ended with the evacuation of Sicily by the Germans and Italians.

The invasion of Sicily finally discredited Mussolini. Once all-powerful, he was now dismissed and arrested. The King, who had made Mussolini Prime Minister back in 1922, told him: 'You are the most hated man in Italy; you have not a single friend left except for me.' Mussolini's successor, Marshal Badoglio, at once began to negotiate with the Allies—a delicate business, since there were still many German divisions in Italy. In the meantime the Allies decided to carry the war to the mainland. British and Canadian troops crossed the Straits of Messina on 3 September, and six days later the Americans landed further up the west coast, at Salerno. By that time, Italy had surrendered. Could the end be in sight?

Roosevelt and Churchill make a statement to journalists at the Casablanca conference.

American troops landing on Italy's west coast in September 1943.

7 VICTORY IN EUROPE

The Germans reacted promptly to the surrender of Italy. They held the Americans long enough at Salerno for the German army to take over most of Italy from their ex-allies. They executed a daring glider-borne rescue of Mussolini, who was installed as leader of a revived Fascist state in northern Italy. And they dug in along a line south of Rome—the Gustave Line—which they held for almost five

Allied landing craft bringing men and equipment ashore at Anzio.

months. They even coped with an Anglo-American landing on the coast further north, at Anzio, pinning down the Allies on their beachhead. The main battle then raged around the ancient mountain monastery of Cassino, which was reduced to rubble by Allied bombing and doggedly defended by the Germans. The Gustave Line broke only in May 1944; a Polish corps stormed Cassino, and on 4 June 1944 Rome was liberated.

By this time the Italian campaign had become a sideshow. Weakened by transfers of troops to France, the Allied forces made only slow progress against an enemy determined to exploit the mountainous terrain and a series of defensible riverlines. As late as April 1945 the Germans were holding on to a substantial part of northern Italy.

The Russians too found that, despite Stalingrad and Kursk, the Germans had plenty of fight left. But although they did not break,

Stalin, Roosevelt and Churchill at the conference in Teheran.

Russian superiority in men and materials forced them to retreat in all sectors. By April 1944 the Red Army had virtually liberated Russian soil and was poised to invade Romania and Poland.

In November 1943 the 'Big Three'—Roosevelt, Churchill and Stalin met for the first time at Teheran, where they made final plans for victory. An invasion in the West and an all-out offensive in the East would squeeze Nazi Germany to death.

The Normandy landings

By June 1944 the Allies had air and naval superiority as well as an advantage in men and materials. All the same, an invasion of Europe, bristling with German guns, mines and other anti-invasion devices, was a formidable undertaking. Among the problems was that of port facilities, which were vitally necessary if the beachheads were to be

With the beach secured, troops and supplies are despatched inland after the D-day landings.

*Captured German soldiers are marched past the Arc de Triomphe after
the liberation of the French capital.*

reinforced—and, as the disastrous Canadian raid on Dieppe had
shown in August 1942, the idea of seizing an existing port was
impractical.

The Allies had spent years in preparation for 'Operation Overlord'.

Incredible masses of men and resources were accumulated in south-east England. An elaborate intelligence network fed a stream of misinformation to the Germans. Air strikes concentrated on the French communications system to disrupt German troop movements. The final decision was made by the American General Dwight D. Eisenhower, Allied Supreme Commander in Europe, who had already proved himself an organizer of genius: 6 June 1944 would be D-day.

Thousands of ships crossed the English Channel, carrying armies, vehicles, stores, and a new invention—artificial harbours, called 'Mulberries'. The Allies landed on five beaches, code-named Omaha, Utah, Gold, Juno and Sword, and dropped airborne troops inland to secure bridgeheads. Taken by surprise and heavily pounded from the air, the Germans responded uncertainly. The battle for the beach-heads was quickly won, though the Americans took heavy casualties on Omaha beach.

Then, despite air-strikes and risings by the French Resistance, the Germans managed to bring up heavy reinforcements. But after fierce fighting the Allies overwhelmed the Germans and broke out of Normandy at the end of July. This was decisive. The campaign that followed bore some resemblance to the German victory of 1940, and was even more successful. Paris was liberated on 19 August by Resistance fighters and Free French soldiers, and by September 1944 France and Belgium had been cleared. Then the offensive came to a halt in the face of Germany's 'Westwall' defensive system, although Montgomery made a daring but unsuccessful attempt to outflank it by seizing Dutch river crossings with airborne troops and thrusting across the Rhine. Failure left the British 1st Airborne Division stranded at Arnhem, where its losses were very serious.

Shortly after the Normandy landings, the Soviet armies swept into Poland. In August the Poles rose against the Germans in Warsaw and took the city, but the Russians could not or would not help them. After a fierce two-month battle the Germans crushed the rising, destroying much of Warsaw in the process. Meanwhile the Axis position in the Balkans crumbled. Romania and Bulgaria capitulated, the Germans abandoned Greece, and Yugoslavia was liberated by Tito's partisans and the Red Army. The Axis forces hung on grimly in Warsaw and Budapest, though the final outcome of the war could hardly be in doubt.

Germany in ruins

And yet the Germans fought on. Hitler himself had nothing to lose; but the discipline—or fanaticism—of the German army and people was extraordinary. Only a small group of conspirators, spurred by the Normandy landings, tried to assassinate Hitler and seize power. This

A statue stands in the midst of the ruins of Dresden.

attempt, known as the 'July Plot', failed, and was followed by horrible Nazi reprisals.

Though purged, the army remained loyal. When Hitler demanded a surprise offensive through the Ardennes to 'smash the Americans completely', new divisions were scraped together and set in motion. The Battle of the Bulge (December 1944) was the last major German offensive. After temporary successes, the Germans were defeated by overwhelming Allied land and air power. Worse, their last reserves were gone.

In January 1945 the Russians invaded Germany, and in February the Western Allies began their final offensive, crossing the Rhine in the following month. Allied bombers ranged over Germany without opposition. Years of intensive bombing had reduced German cities to rubble and, it was believed, crippled the German war effort. But this was later found to have been an illusion: as in Britain, morale was only stiffened by civilian deaths, while German war production actually peaked in 1944. In February 1945, Dresden, a beautiful old city of no military value, was utterly destroyed by bombing; the 60,000 deaths there have often been described as one of the Allies' 'war crimes'.

Hitler still hoped for a miracle. From June 1944 new weapons had been launched against Britain—the V–1 'flying bomb' and the V–2, the first missile. They came too late to effect the issue. Hopes that the Allies would fall out proved far-fetched. Russian and American troops

A V-1 in flight. These jet-propelled 'flying bombs' destroyed 25,000 houses and killed 6,000 people in London.

GEN. ROOKS

JODL

DOENITZ

VON FRIEDEBURG

Following Germany's surrender, Admiral Doenitz, General Jodl and Admiral von Friedeburg are told that they are prisoners of war. Von Friedeburg later committed suicide, and Doenitz and Jodl were tried as war criminals.

met on the River Elbe, cutting Germany in two. In Italy, German resistance collapsed at last. Mussolini was captured and shot by partisans. The Russians stormed into Berlin. On 30 April Hitler killed himself, to 'escape the disgrace of deposition or capitulation,' leaving the navy chief, Doenitz, to authorize the formal surrender on 8 May 1945—VE (Victory in Europe) Day.

8 THE WAR AGAINST JAPAN

Japan struck at Pearl Harbor because the United States was the chief obstacle to Japanese expansion. The colonial powers in the Far East—Britain, France and the Netherlands—were entirely absorbed in the European war and incapable of assisting their thinly spread forces in Asia. (In fact, French Indo-China was already virtually a Japanese colony.) But the United States had condemned Japan's war on China, and had begun to use economic sanctions against her. Wiping out the Pacific Fleet would leave the United States

The British battleship HMS Repulse, *which was sunk by Japanese aircraft on 10 December 1941.*

General Douglas MacArthur on one of the islands of the Philippines.

powerless to halt the Japanese advance. By the time the Americans recovered, Japan would have a far-flung, easily defensible empire; the cost of defeating it would be so prohibitive that the Americans would settle for a negotiated peace.

These Japanese calculations grossly underestimated the fighting spirit and the enormous resources of the USA. But the immediate result, in terms of the number of American ships and aircraft destroyed, was impressive. On the other hand, three vital ships—the fleet's aircraft carriers—were not in port and escaped destruction.

The Japanese offensive
Simultaneously with their attack on Pearl Harbor, the Japanese launched a successful, multi-pronged drive into Asia and the Pacific. The forces of the British Empire, long regarded as the dominant power in the East, proved to be poorly prepared and co-ordinated.

Two big ships specially sent out from Britain, the *Prince of Wales* and the *Repulse*, were sunk by Japanese planes. Hong Kong capitulated on Christmas Day 1941. The Japanese invaded Malaya from the north and raced through supposedly impenetrable jungle to Singapore, whose powerful defensive guns pointed uselessly out to sea. Singapore was regarded as the great British stronghold in the East, but the Commonwealth forces were thrown into confusion by the speed of the Japanese advance. The island surrendered on 15 February 1942, and 60,000 Allied soldiers went into captivity. Almost all of Burma also fell to the Japanese before the monsoons arrived in May to save the retreating British. Meanwhile, in March, a hastily assembled Anglo-American-Australian-Dutch fleet was destroyed by the Japanese navy at the battle of the Java Sea. In the Philippines, American troops under General Douglas MacArthur did a little—but only a little—better, holding on at Bataan and Corregidor until May.

South-east Asia offered Japan oil, rice, rubber and other commodities she lacked. Her conquests in the Western Pacific had another motive: to create a defensive perimeter far out in the ocean against American retaliation. Apart from a heroic but short-lived resistance by American troops on Wake Island, the Japanese had little trouble in taking the Marianas, Marshalls and Gilberts.

In six months Japan had launched a series of victorious 3,000-mile offensives, and had created an empire stretching from Burma to the Marshalls. The Japanese preferred to call it the 'Greater Asia Co-Prosperity Sphere', and won some support by posing as anti-white and anti-colonialist. But like Hitler's New Order, the Japanese 'Sphere' was run for the benefit of the occupying power and was soon seen to represent, at best, no more than a change of masters.

Setbacks

The first Japanese failures occurred in New Guinea. Initially they swept along the north coast and into the Solomon Islands. But their advance across the island to Port Moresby was stopped by the Australians, and an intended naval attack on the town was checked at the battle of the Coral Sea. This was the first sea battle in which the opposed fleets never caught sight of each other: carrier-borne aircraft fought it out and bombed the ships of the other side.

Air power was a crucial factor on both land and sea, but the vast Pacific distances—far beyond the fuel capacity of planes—made it dependent on possession of aircraft carriers. For this reason, the battle of Midway in June 1942 was of vital importance. Pushing out further into the Pacific, the Japanese were surprised by the Americans, and in the battle that followed four carriers were lost, seriously weakening

American aircraft carriers leading a line of battleships in the Pacific.

the Japanese capacity to hold their scattered conquests. However, as part of the offensive they did land on the Aleutian Islands—the last of their conquests and the only US soil they were ever to hold.

The crumbling empire

After Midway, the advantage in the Pacific passed to the Allies, as the battle for Guadalcanal in the Solomons confirmed. Beginning in August·1942 with the US Marines' assault to capture the island's airfield, this developed into the great slogging match of the Pacific war, with both sides pouring in troops, ships and planes. Fortunes fluctuated in the series of fierce naval engagements that accompanied the land battle, which ended only with a Japanese withdrawal in

American troops during landing operations on Guadalcanal.

US Marines hunt for Japanese snipers hiding on a recaptured Pacific island.

February 1943.

As elsewhere, the Allies' ability to replace, and more than replace, their losses was a decisive factor. By contrast, the depletion of Japan's merchant shipping, her carrier losses, and the elimination of her trained pilots grew increasingly serious. Japan was nowhere near as strong as Nazi Germany, but her resistance was protracted by the fact that the Allies' priority was the war in Europe, and by the sheer distances and difficulties of terrain involved in the Allied counter-offensives. The fanaticism instilled by the Japanese military code was also important. If they could not withdraw, Japanese soldiers fought to the death rather than surrender; their commanders usually committed ritual suicide, *harakiri*. Thus every Allied advance was held up by futile resistance culminating in a massacre.

Their military code was also responsible for most Japanese atrocities. Since they considered surrender an unthinkable degradation, they treated prisoners of war with infamous cruelty, as creatures beneath civilized consideration.

For most of 1943–44 there were three major theatres in the war against Japan. In the jungles of Burma, British and Commonwealth troops fought hard, indecisive jungle campaigns which turned in the Allies' favour only late in 1944, enabling them to open the 'Burma Road' to China and link up with Chinese and American forces. In New Guinea, American and Australian combined operations (land, sea and air), brilliantly directed by MacArthur, brought the Allies within striking distance of the Philippines. And in the Pacific the US Navy

63

and Marines conducted an 'island hopping' campaign which took them through the Gilberts, Marshalls, Marianas and Carolines in a series of spectacular amphibious assaults. In June 1944 a Japanese attempt to ambush the American fleet in the Marianas was anticipated and met with overwhelming force. The battle of the Philippine Sea became, in service slang, the 'Marianas Turkey Shoot', reflecting the wholesale slaughter of Japanese planes which made their carriers useless and left their navy hopelessly vulnerable to attack.

In October, MacArthur redeemed the promise he had made on leaving the Philippines in 1942—'I shall return.' The conquest of the Philippines was ruinous for the Japanese; it cut their empire in two, and a desperate attempt to beat off the Allied landings only led to the destruction of the Japanese navy at the battle of Leyte Gulf.

Raising the American flag on Mount Suribachi, Iwo Jima, marking the island's capture from the Japanese.

The ruins of Hiroshima, viewed from the highest building left standing by the atomic blast.

The final act

From November 1944, long-distance bombing missions by American B-29 Superfortresses brought the war to Japan. The Allies were now determined to bomb the enemy into submission or directly invade her 'home islands'. Either way, every island conquered brought Japan within range of more bombers. The Japanese knew this, and the American invasion of Iwo Jima in February was a notably bloody struggle. In April it was the turn of Okinawa, the first historic Japanese territory to fall. Beyond dying in appalling numbers (110,000 on Okinawa alone), the Japanese had no answer. The remnants of the Japanese Imperial Navy sailed out with enough fuel for a one-way journey. They were duly sent to the bottom of the Pacific. A final 'secret weapon' caused substantial damage, but not enough to affect the outcome—several thousand *kamikazes*, young suicide pilots who crashed their bomb-filled planes on the decks of American ships.

Japan, with her crowded cities of wooden houses, suffered far more from Allied bombing than Germany had done; one incendiary bomb attack on Tokyo in March 1945 killed about 168,000 people; an observer described how 'a fountain of brilliant sparks rose skyward and in no time the city was in a welter of belching smoke and roaring flames ... In one night the major part of the city was transformed into a vast plain of scorched earth.' But even with their country devastated and their Axis allies defeated, the Japanese would not surrender; given their code, they hardly knew how to. Eventually Harry S. Truman, who had succeeded to the American presidency on

*MacArthur receives the Japanese surrender, which officially ended the
Second World War.*

Roosevelt's death in April 1945, decided that a further invasion would
cost too many Allied lives. He authorized the use of a frightful new
weapon. An atomic bomb was dropped above the city of Hiroshima on
6 August 1945, killing (at the most conservative estimate) 80,000
people and destroying more than half the city. Three days later, a
second bomb, dropped on Nagasaki, decided matters. Japan formally
surrendered on 14 August 1945.

9 THE POST-WAR WORLD

Between September 1939, when German troops invaded Poland, and the surrender of the Japanese in August 1945, the peoples of fifty-seven nations, Allied and Axis, were involved in fighting the Second World War. During this time, national boundaries disappeared, towns and cities were reduced to rubble, and populations were decimated.

The cost
During the war at least 17,000,000 combatants died. Among them were 3,250,000 Germans, 2,000,000 Japanese, 2,000,000 Chinese, 6,000,000 Russians, 400,000 Americans and 250,000 British. Civilian deaths from bombing, starvation and policies of deliberate extermination numbered at least 25,000,000. At the end of the war, much of Europe and Asia lay in ruins, and there were millions of homeless people and refugees. Of the major powers, only the United States, protected by two oceans, remained unscathed and emerged from the war stronger than before.

The cost of raising and maintaining the armed forces was, of course, astronomical; the destruction of homes, industries and means of livelihood of millions of people probably represented an even greater cost.

Post-war reconstruction is outside the scope of this book, but it is worth noticing how much of the modern world is a direct or indirect result of the war.

A new world?
There was a widespread desire for a new international order to ensure peace and fair dealing between nations. International law was invoked to put the Fascist leaders and their followers on trial for war crimes. Many were sentenced to death or imprisonment. More positively, the Atlantic Charter and other wartime meetings led to the setting up of the United Nations Organization as a successor to the League of Nations.

Hopes for a new kind of future influenced the British people in particular. Though Churchill was revered as a war leader, he was

At least 17,000,000 combatants and 25,000,000 civilians died during the war, and vast areas of Europe and Asia were reduced to ruins.

identified with the old order of privilege, poverty and unemployment. In 1945 the Labour Party led by Clement Attlee came to power and proceeded to create the Welfare State which became a fundamental feature of British society.

Many advances in science and technology were by-products of the war effort. Antibiotics were developed for treatment of the wounded. Nuclear power proved to have peaceful as well as destructive possibilities. And V-bombs led on to space flight as well as missiles.

The Iron Curtain

The size and resources of the USA and USSR ensured that they would emerge from the war as the new 'superpowers'. Communist regimes were installed in Poland, Czechoslovakia and most other states liberated by the Red Army, and Russian-occupied East Germany also became a Communist state, separate from the Federal Republic (West Germany). As relations between the superpowers deteriorated, the

United States and western Europe formed a military alliance (NATO) which was confronted by a Communist equivalent (the Warsaw Pact). The 'Iron Curtain' now dividing Europe still follows fairly closely the line of the furthest Russian advance in Europe during the Second World War.

A new Europe
European recovery could only be achieved by co-operation between former enemies. It was given all the more willingly as the old rivalries began to seem absurd in a world no longer dominated by Europe. And Europeans found the idea of 'Europe' more attractive with the more

Churchill receives the cheers of the crowds on VE Day—8 May 1945. He was defeated by Clement Attlee in the general election held less than three months later.

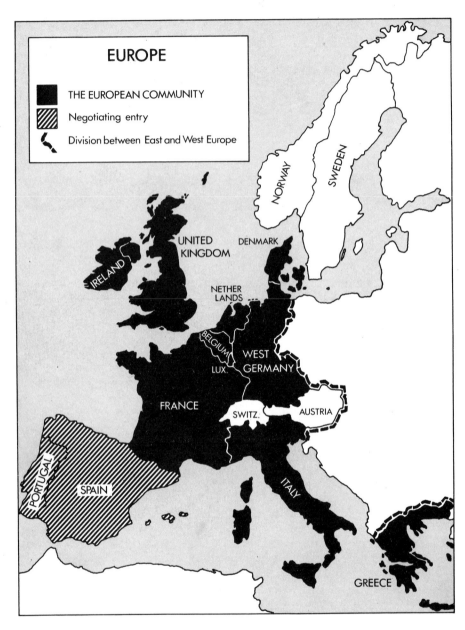

EUROPE

■ THE EUROPEAN COMMUNITY

▨ Negotiating entry

Division between East and West Europe

NORWAY
SWEDEN

UNITED KINGDOM
DENMARK
IRELAND
NETHER LANDS
BELGIUM
WEST GERMANY
LUX.
FRANCE
SWITZ.
AUSTRIA
PORTUGAL
SPAIN
ITALY
GREECE

The Common Market, or European Economic Community.

or less painful dismantling of the colonial empires—itself in part a result of the war, which shattered the myth of white invincibility. The result was the emergence of the Common Market (EEC) and the possibility that Europe might become an independent force.

The mushroom cloud rises 20,000 feet into the air after the Nagasaki atomic bomb. Today's nuclear weapons are far more powerful than those used during the Second World War.

'The Bomb'

The development of nuclear weapons may prove to be the worst of all legacies of the Second World War. The writer Arthur Koestler suggested that Hiroshima marked the beginning of a new age in history—the age in which humanity must live with the knowledge that it can destroy itself.

71

GLOSSARY

Armistice An agreement between opposing armies to stop fighting in order to discuss peace terms, often, in effect, terms of surrender

Communism A political ideology or system which aims to bring about a society without social classes, in which private ownership is abolished and the means of production belong to the community as a whole.

Demilitarize To remove all military personnel and equipment from an area.

Fascism A militaristic right-wing, nationalist ideology with an authoritarian structure, opposed to democracy and liberalism.

Great Depression The world-wide economic slump of the early 1930s which brought about mass unemployment.

Isolationism A policy of withdrawal from international affairs.

Liberty ships Supply ships used during the Second World War; many were specially constructed in the USA.

Maginot Line The line of fortifications built by France to defend its border with Germany. It was named after André Maginot, the French minister of war when the fortifications were begun in 1929.

Nazi A member of the National Socialist German Workers' Party which seized power in Germany in 1933 under Adolf Hitler.

Panzers Fast mechanized armoured units used by the German army. The word Panzer is also sometimes used to describe a German tank of the Second World War.

Partisan A member of a group of armed resistance fighters within occupied territory.

The Resistance An illegal organization fighting for national liberty in a country occupied by an enemy.

PICTURE ACKNOWLEDGEMENTS

The illustrations in this book were supplied by: Bundesarchiv 19; Imperial War Museum, London *front cover*, 10, 11, 13, 15, 16, 17, 20, 22, 23, 24, 26, 27, 29, 35, 39, 40, 41, 42, 44, 48, 50, 51, 53, 56, 65, 68, 69, 71; PHOTRI 34, 52, 59, 62, 63; Popperfoto 4, 5, 14, 18, 21, 33, 37, 38, 43, 45, 47, 49, 55, 57, 58, 61, 64, 66; Malcolm S. Walker 12. The remaining pictures are from the Wayland Picture Library.

DATE CHART

1939
1 Sept　　Nazi Germany invades Poland
3 Sept　　Britain and France declare war on Germany
Nov–Dec　　Russo-Finnish war
13 Dec　　*Graf Spee* scuttled

1940
9 Apr　　German invasion of Norway and Denmark
10 May　　Germans begin invasion of Low Countries and France; Churchill becomes British Prime Minister
May–early June　　Dunkirk
10 June　　Italy enters the war
22 June　　France signs Armistice
Aug–Nov　　Battle of Britain at its height
28 Oct　　Italy invades Greece
Dec–Mar 1941　　Italian collapse in Greece and East Africa

1941
11 Mar　　Lend-Lease Act
Apr　　Germans conquer Yugoslavia and Greece; Rommel's first offensive in North Africa
27 May　　Sinking of *Bismarck*
22 June　　Germans invade the Soviet Union
7 Dec　　Japanese attack Pearl Harbor

1942
Feb　　Fall of Singapore; Battle of the Java Sea
4–8 May　　Battle of the Coral Sea
May–July　　Rommel's second offensive in North Africa
30 May　　'Thousand bomber raid' on Cologne
4 June　　Battle of Midway
Aug–Feb 1943　　Battle of Guadalcanal
Oct–Nov　　Battle of El Alamein
Nov　　Allied invasion of French North Africa; Germans move into Vichy France

1943
Feb　　Germans capitulate at Stalingrad
July　　Invasion of Sicily; fall of Mussolini
Sept　　Surrender of Italy; Germans free Mussolini and occupy north of Italy

1944
6 June　　D-day
June　　Battle of the Philippine Sea
20 July　　Unsuccessful 'July Plot' against Hitler
Aug–Oct　　Warsaw Rising
17–26 Sept　　Battle of Arnhem
16–25 Dec　　Battle of the Bulge

1945		8 May	Surrender of Germany
Feb	Americans land on Iwo Jima	6 Aug	First atomic bomb dropped on Hiroshima
Apr	Americans land on Okinawa	9 Aug	Atomic bomb dropped on Nagasaki
28 Apr	Death of Mussolini		
30 Apr	Death of Hitler	14 Aug	Surrender of Japan

FURTHER READING

Allen, Kenneth *Battle of the Atlantic* Wayland, 1973
Bullock, Alan *Hitler: a study in tyranny* Pelican, 1962
Calder, Angus *The People's War: Britain 1939–45* Cape, 1969
Clark, Alan *Barbarossa: the Russian-German conflict, 1941–45* Hutchinson, 1965
Deighton, Len *Fighter* Triad/Granada, 1979
Gilbert, Martin *Final Journey: the fate of the Jews in Nazi Europe* Allen and Unwin, 1979
Hersey, John *Hiroshima* Knopf, 1946
Hobbs, Anthony *The Battle of Britain* Wayland, 1973
Holden, Matthew *The Desert Rats* Wayland, 1973
Parkinson, Roger *The Origins of World War Two* Wayland, 1970
Robertson, E. M. (ed.) *The Origins of the Second World War: historical interpretations* Macmillan, 1971
Ryan, Cornelius *The Longest Day* Gollancz, 1960
Shirer, William L. *The Rise and Fall of the Third Reich* Pan, 1964
Smith, Denis Mack *Mussolini* Weidenfeld, 1981
Stokesbury, James L. *A Short History of World War II* Hale, 1982
Taylor, A. J. P. *The Origins of the Second World War* Hamish Hamilton, 1961

Memoirs and documents
Churchill, Winston S. *The Second World War* (abridged memoirs) Cassell, 1959
de Gaulle, Charles *War Memoirs* Collins, 1955
The Diary of Anne Frank Pan, 1954
Keneally, Thomas *Schindler's Ark* Hodder and Stoughton, 1982
Montgomery, Bernard *Memoirs* Collins, 1960
Spears, Sir Edward *Assignment to Catastrophe* Heinemann, 1954

INDEX

60408